PICTURES OFF THE WALL

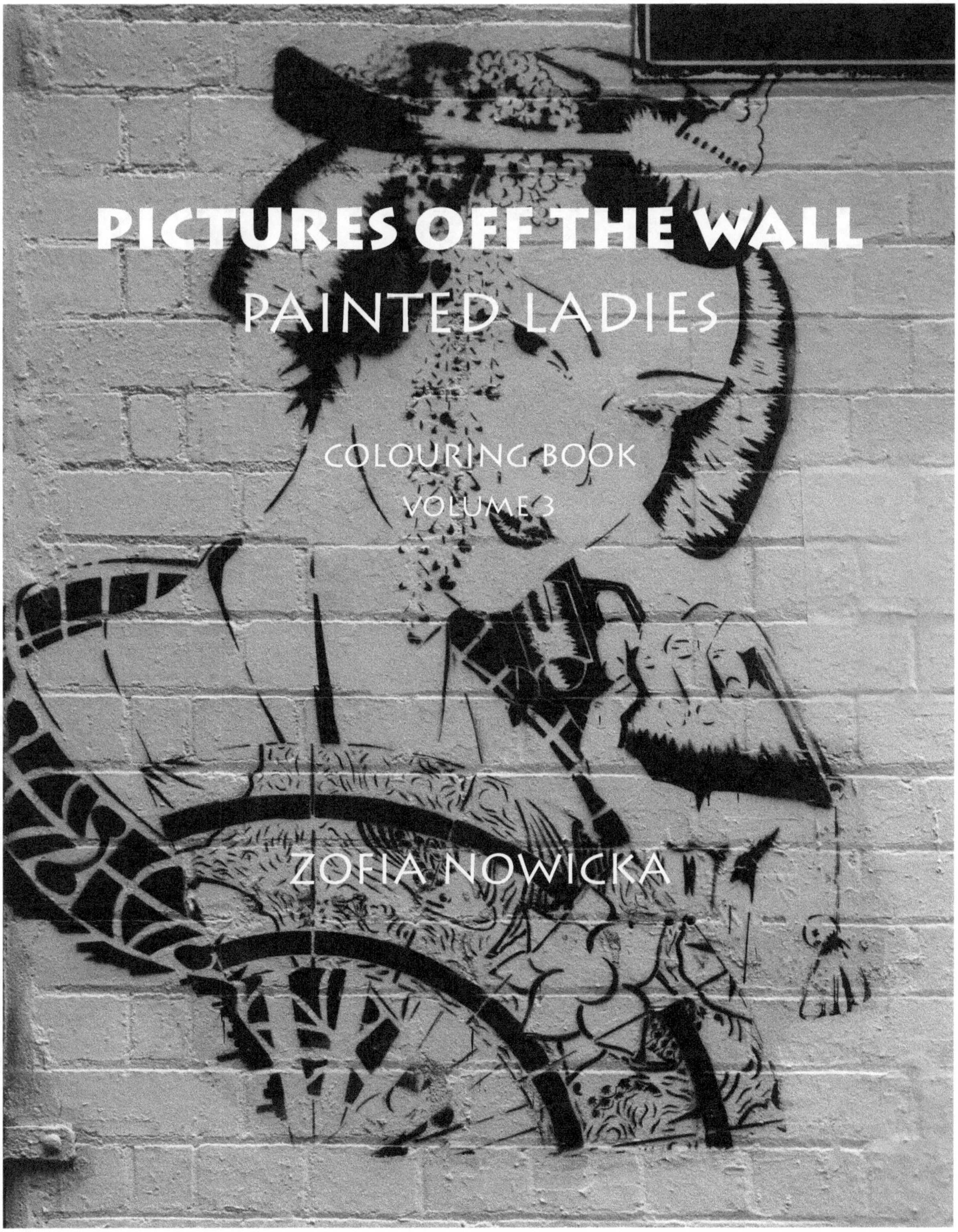

PAINTED LADIES

COLOURING BOOK
VOLUME 3

ZOFIA NOWICKA

Pictures Off The Wall Series

·PICTURES OFF THE WALL BOOK
·PICTURES OFF THE WALL - LITTLE CREATURES BOOK
·PICTURES OFF THE WALL - PAINTED LADIES BOOK

www.picturesoffthewall.com

PICTURES OFF THE WALL
PAINTED LADIES

Walk with me and explore Melbourne's famous street art and graffiti in the city's labyrinth of lanes.
Melbourne is famous for its arcades and laneways. There are many hidden art works tucked around street corners, little surprises waiting to be discovered. Secret passages leading to outdoor urban art galleries. It's very Melbourne.
As Banksy said about melbourne's graffiti:
'Australia's most significant contribution to the arts since they stole the Aborigine's pencils'.

Of course, the nature of street art is that it's forever changing, so to record it, one has to be fast.
I spent days ducking down the alleys stepping over bins and taking a lot of photographs of official and less official pieces of inspiration. I selected 27 images and compiled them in a book of graffiti to be hand coloured in infinite ways.

Zofia Nowicka

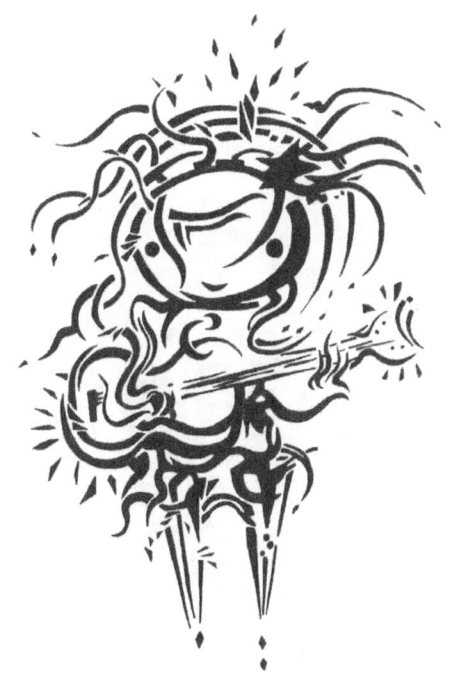

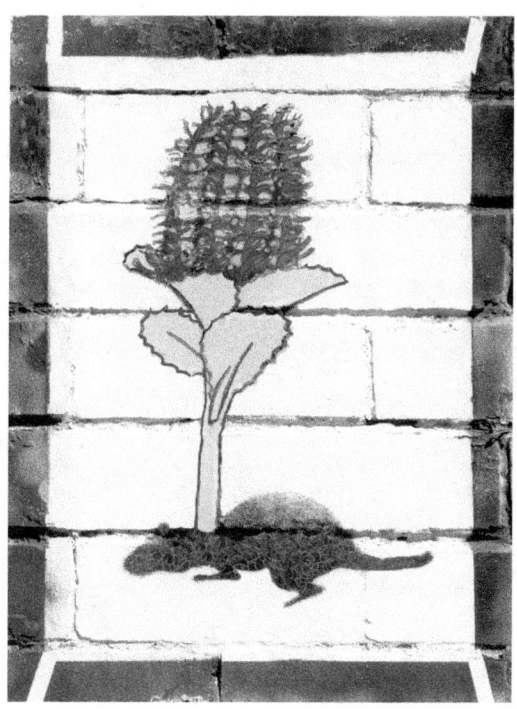

www.picturesoffthewall.com

Zofia Nowicka is a Melbourne based artist working in digital photography, sculpture
and drawings. Originally graduating from Lodz Art School in Poland she migrated to
Australia and continued her craft as a visual
artist. She also ran an art gallery and recently completed her Masters degree from
the Victorian College of the Arts. She continues to exhibit her own work and her latest
project is the book of Melbourne graffiti art, titled 'Pictures Off The Wall'. Zofia utilises
her photographic and artistic experience to capture and transform found images into
little masterpieces. People of all ages will have a lot of fun colouring the Walls!

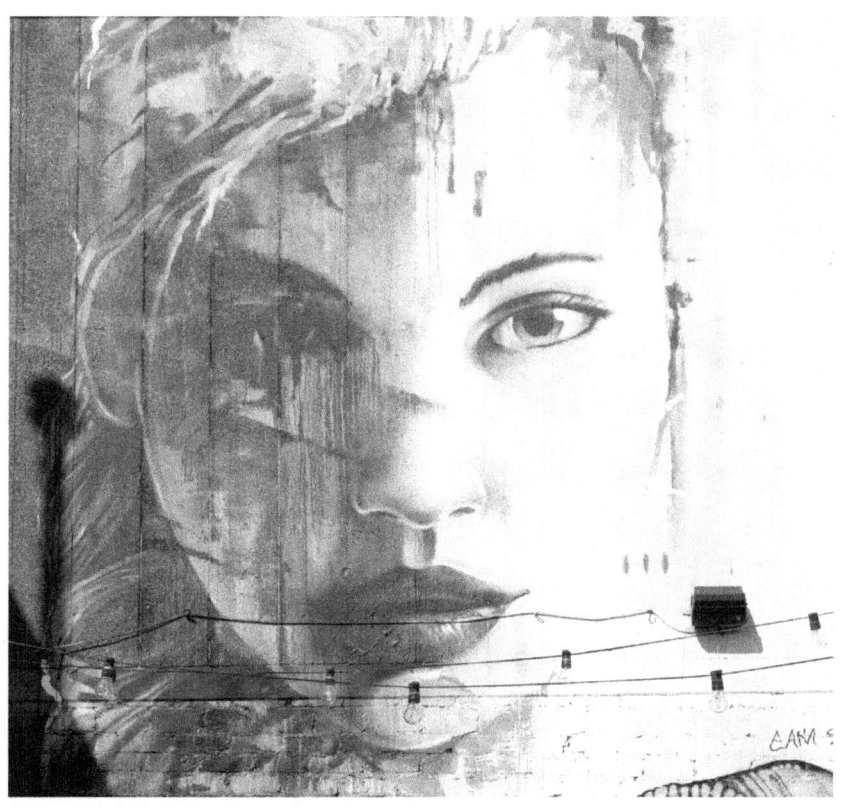

Painted Ladies look at us from walls of Melbourne lanes. Some look pensive, immersed in
their world. Others are feminine, sexy, and skittish. Polka-dots pants, high heels, red Vespa,
blue dress, black hair flowing in the wind and her hand in an elegant glove.
Little ballerina suspended in a pirouette. Cool mint ice-cream, pink harts floating above,
amorous cat. And then the fat lady singing …stop and listen.
Beautiful women— bring them to life with colour.

The images in this book are suitable for colour pencils markers and
variety of other colouring media. For these illustrations I think colour pencils
are better for blending colours, tones, shadows and light. I have included
couple of blank pages to test the colours.

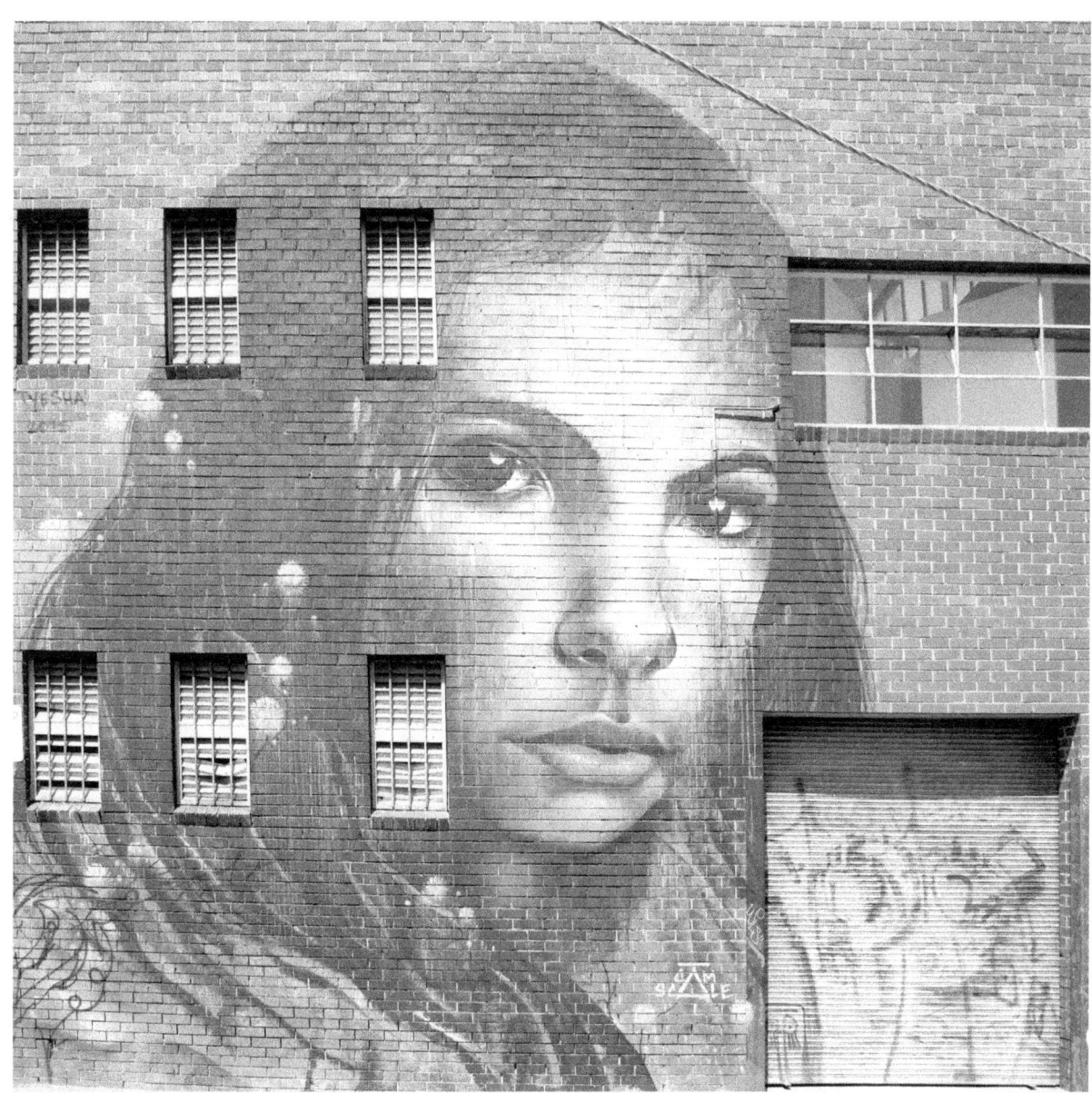

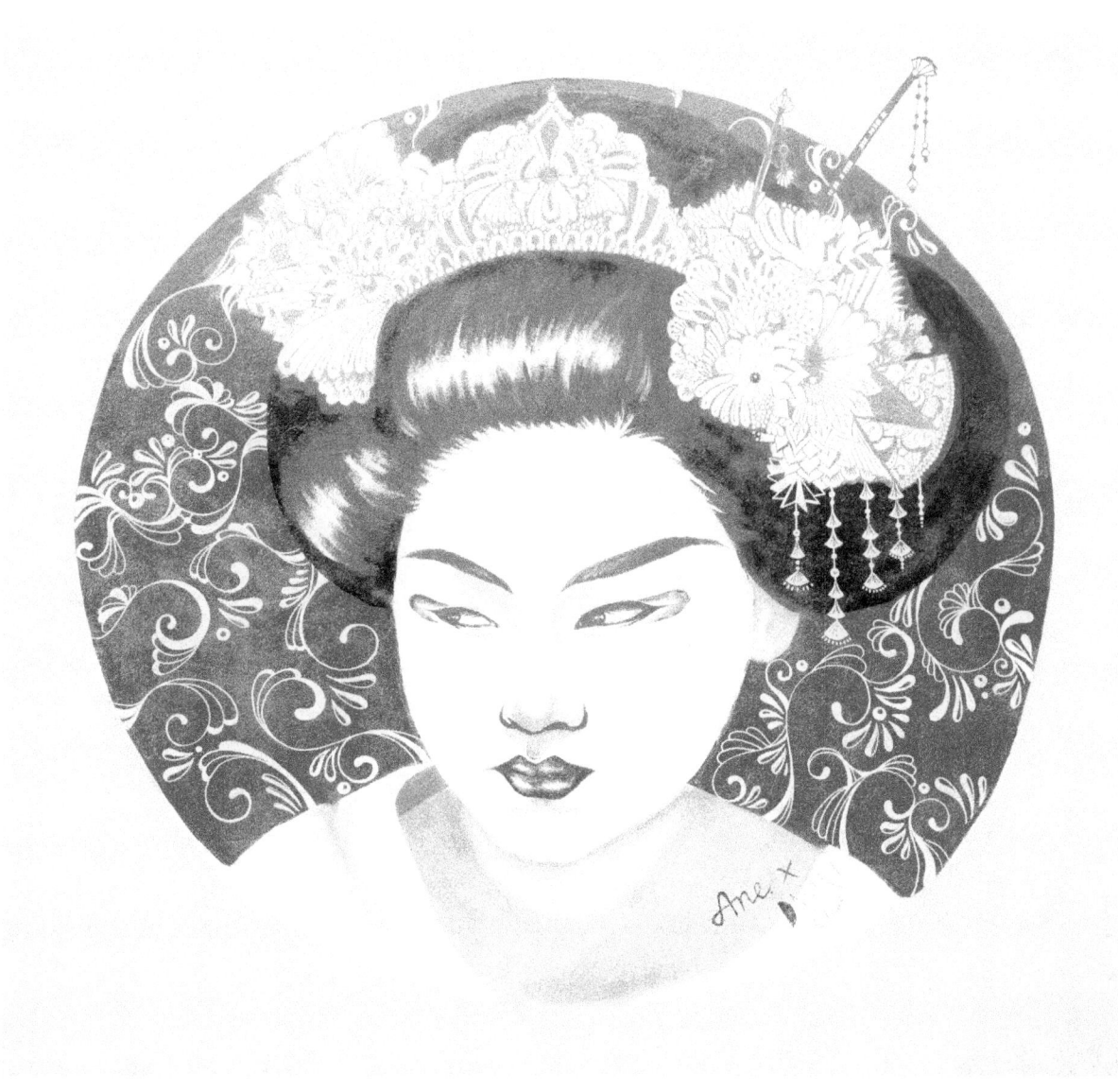

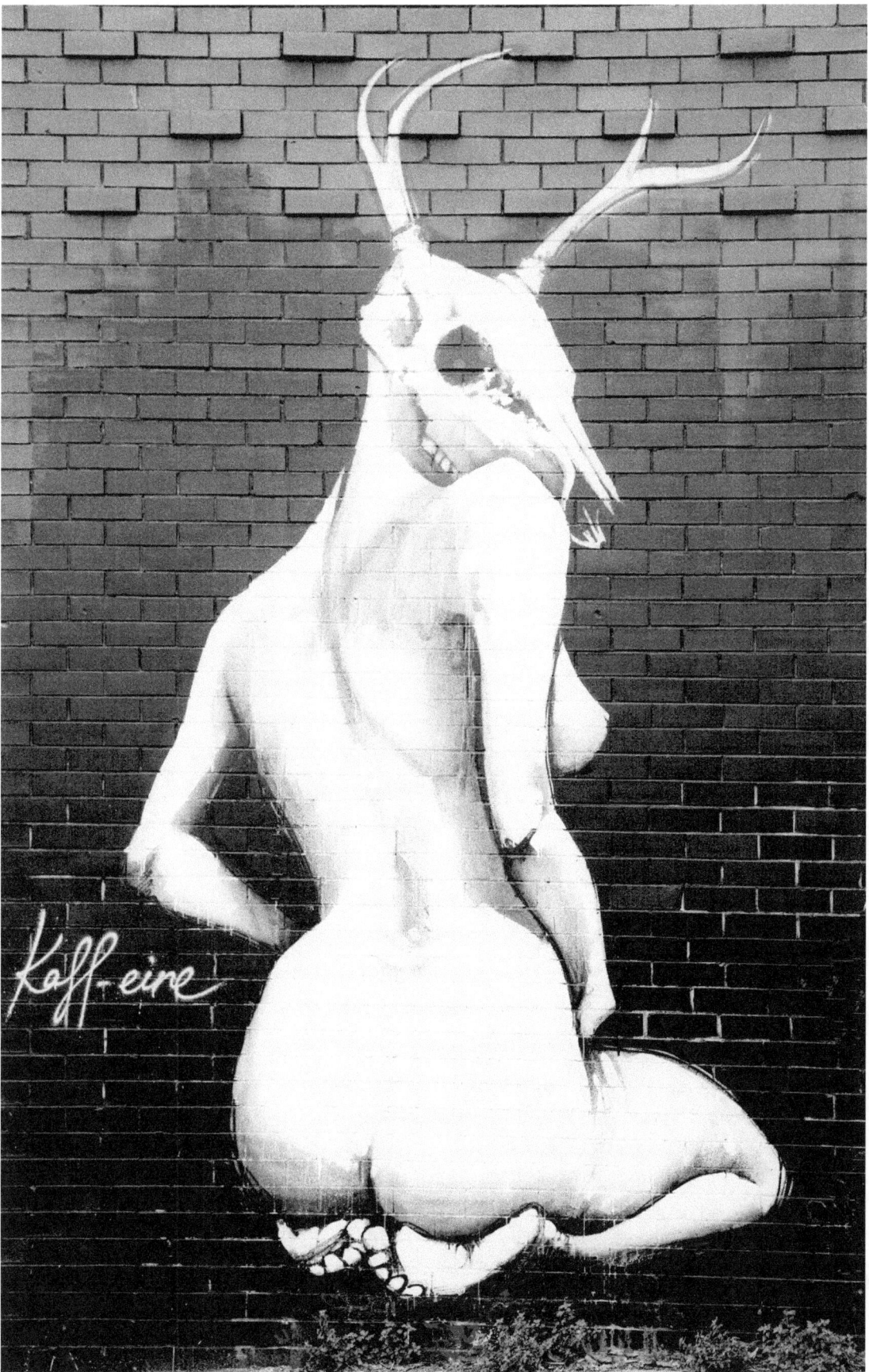

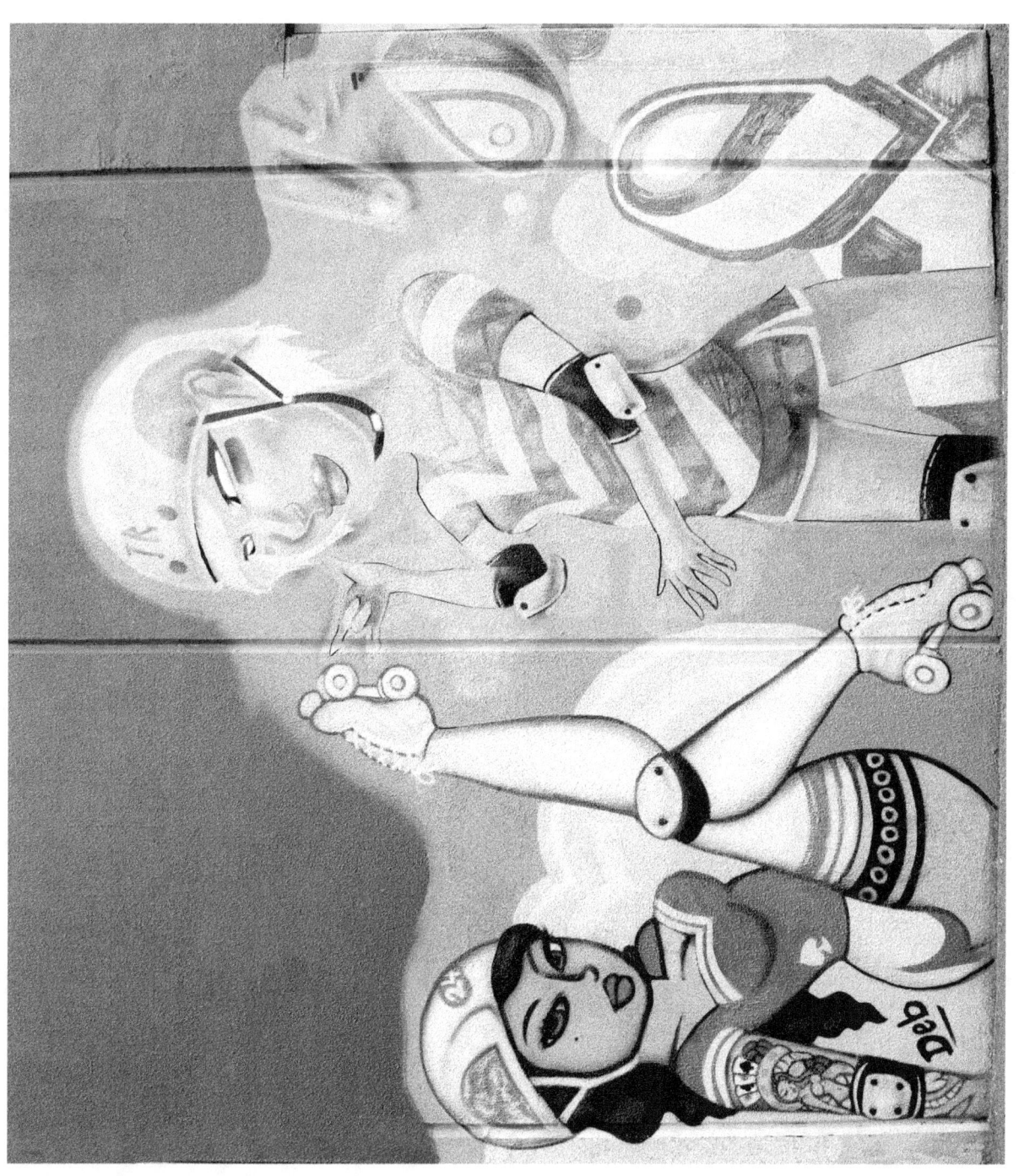

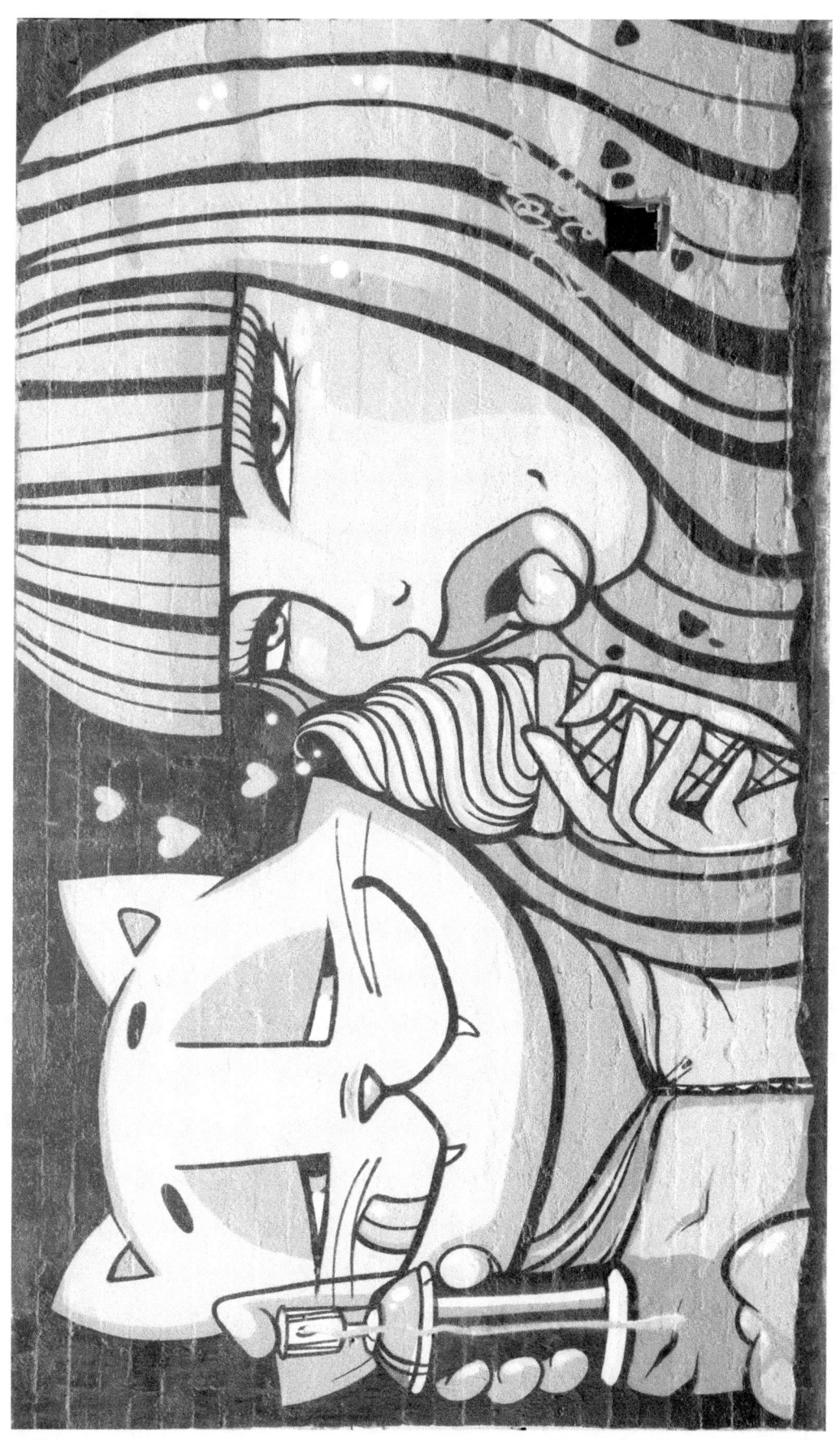

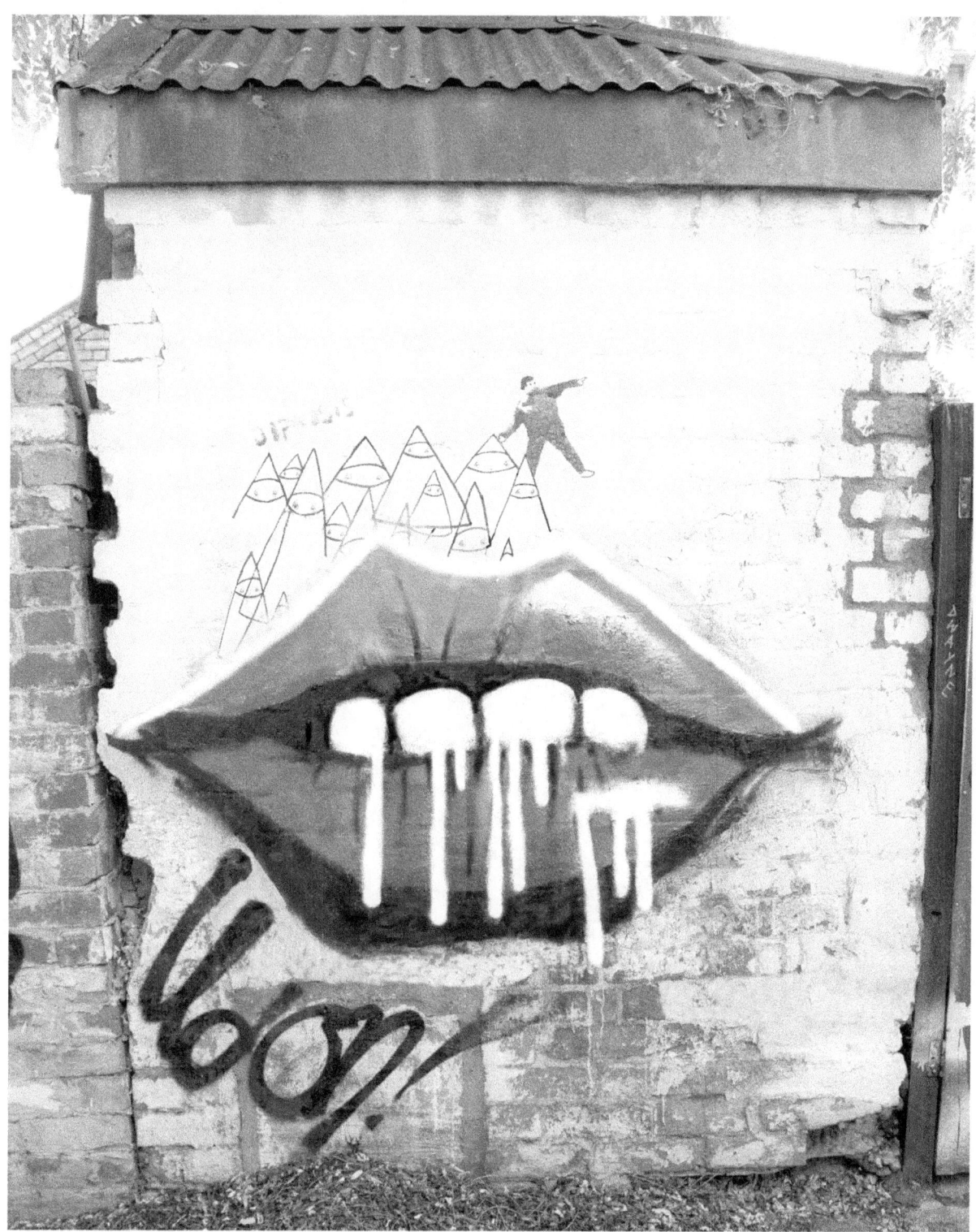

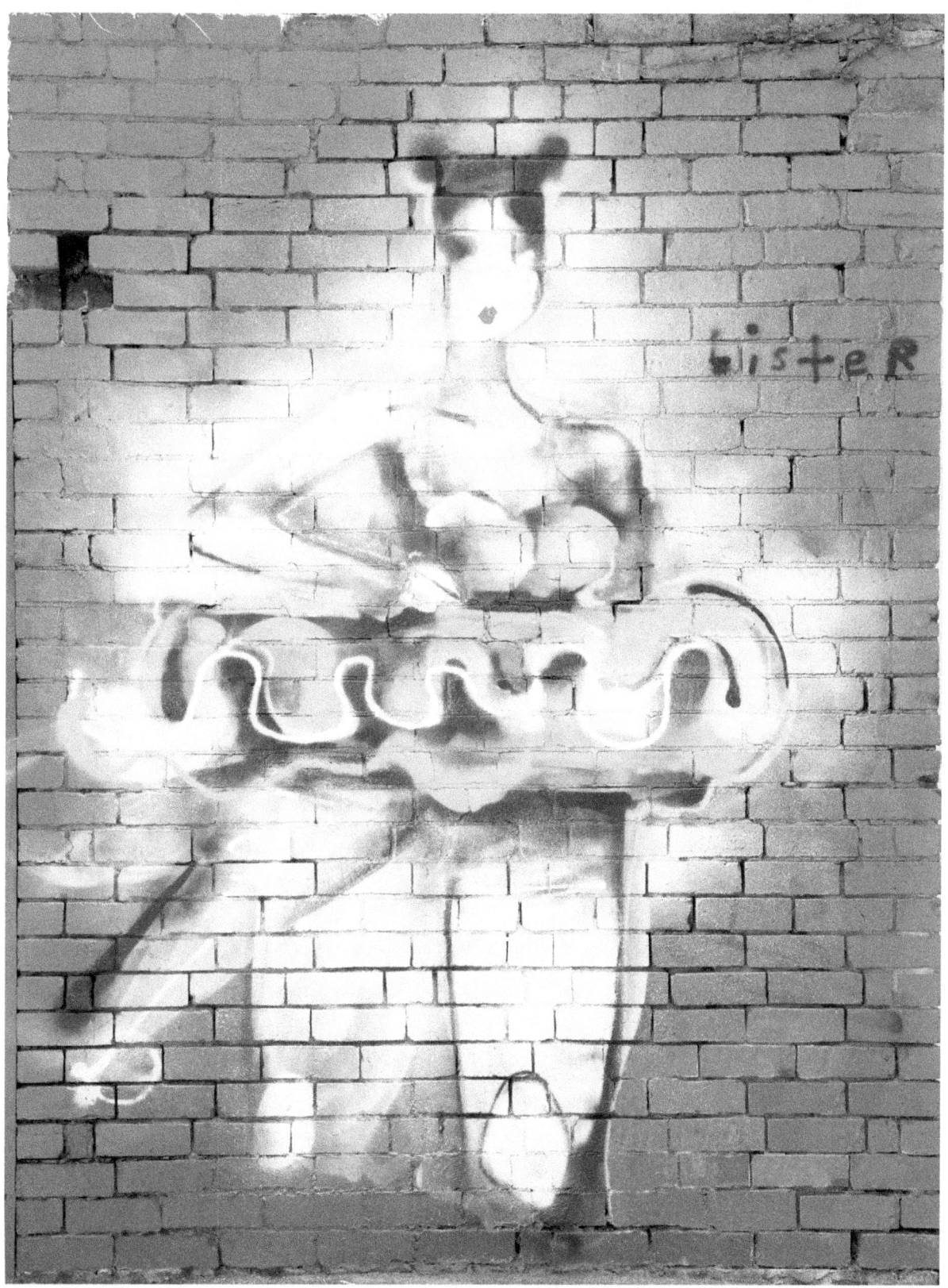

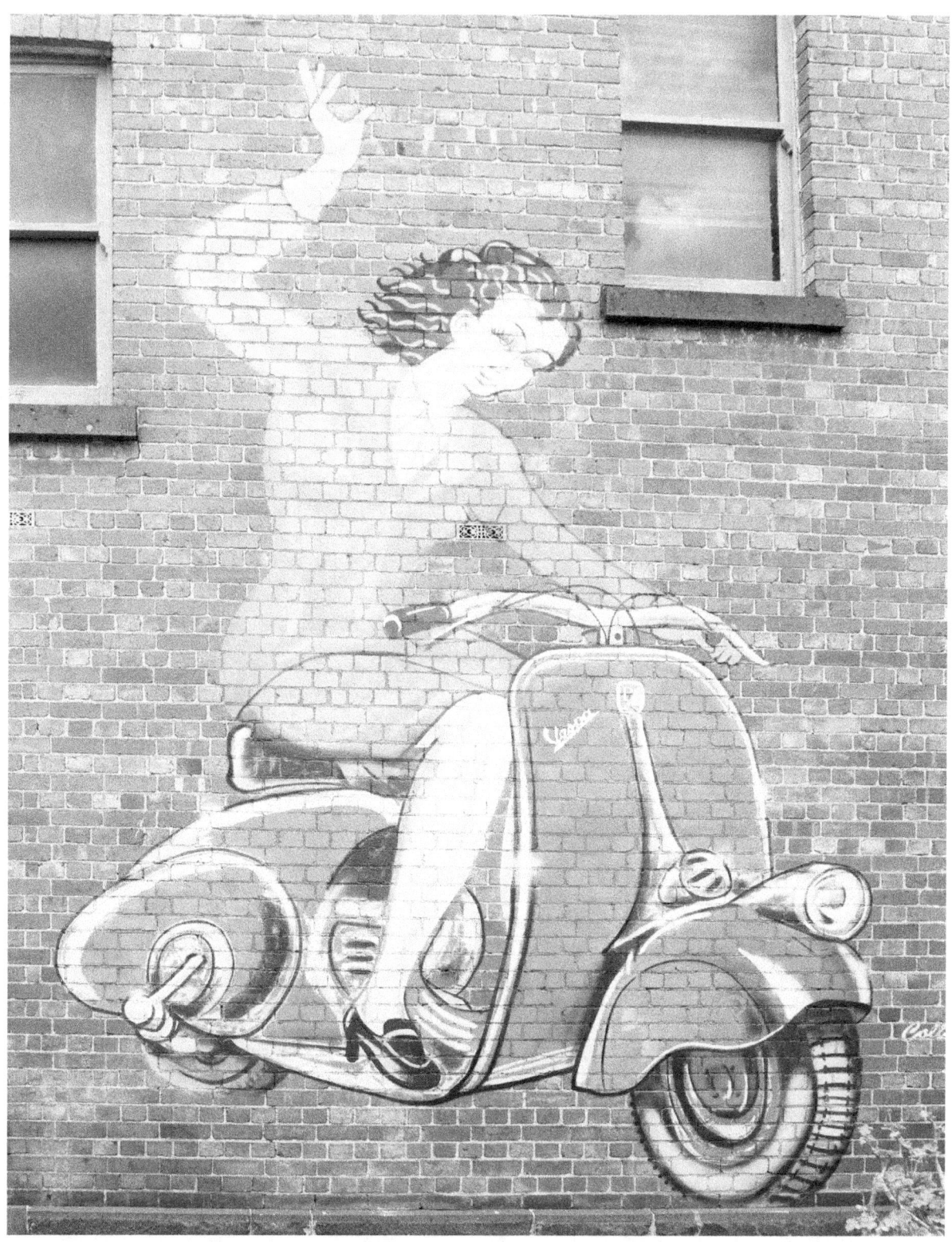

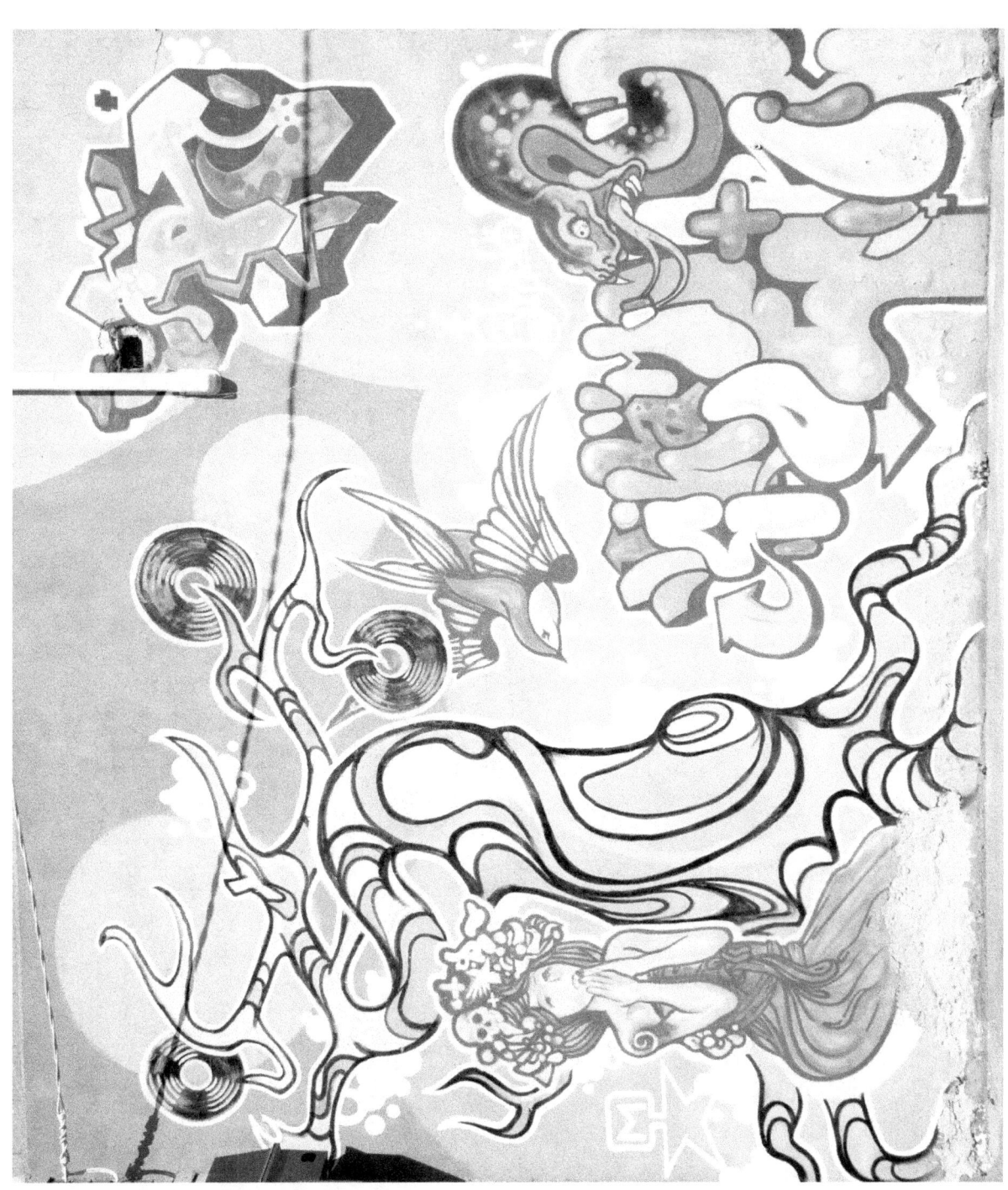

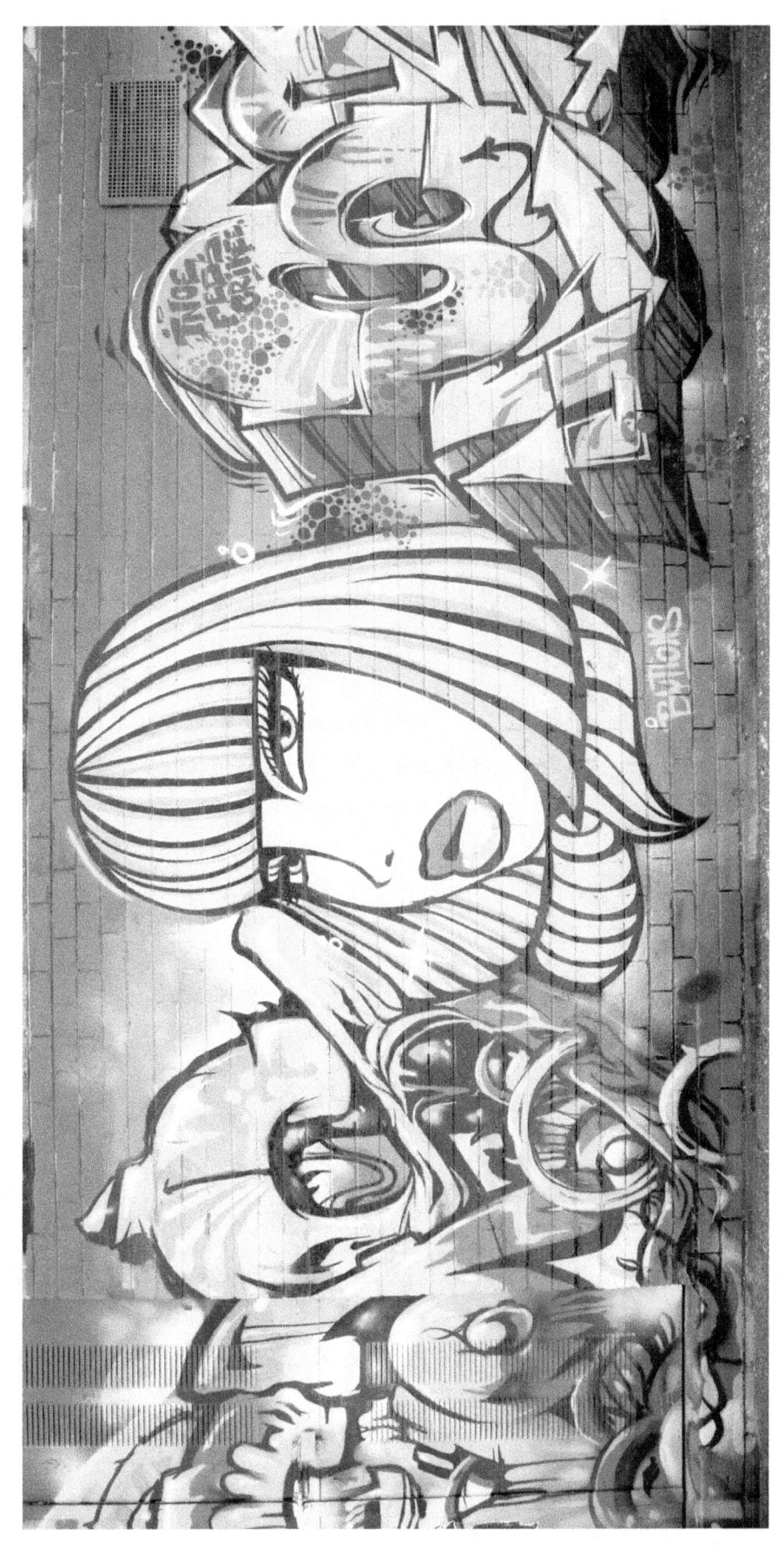

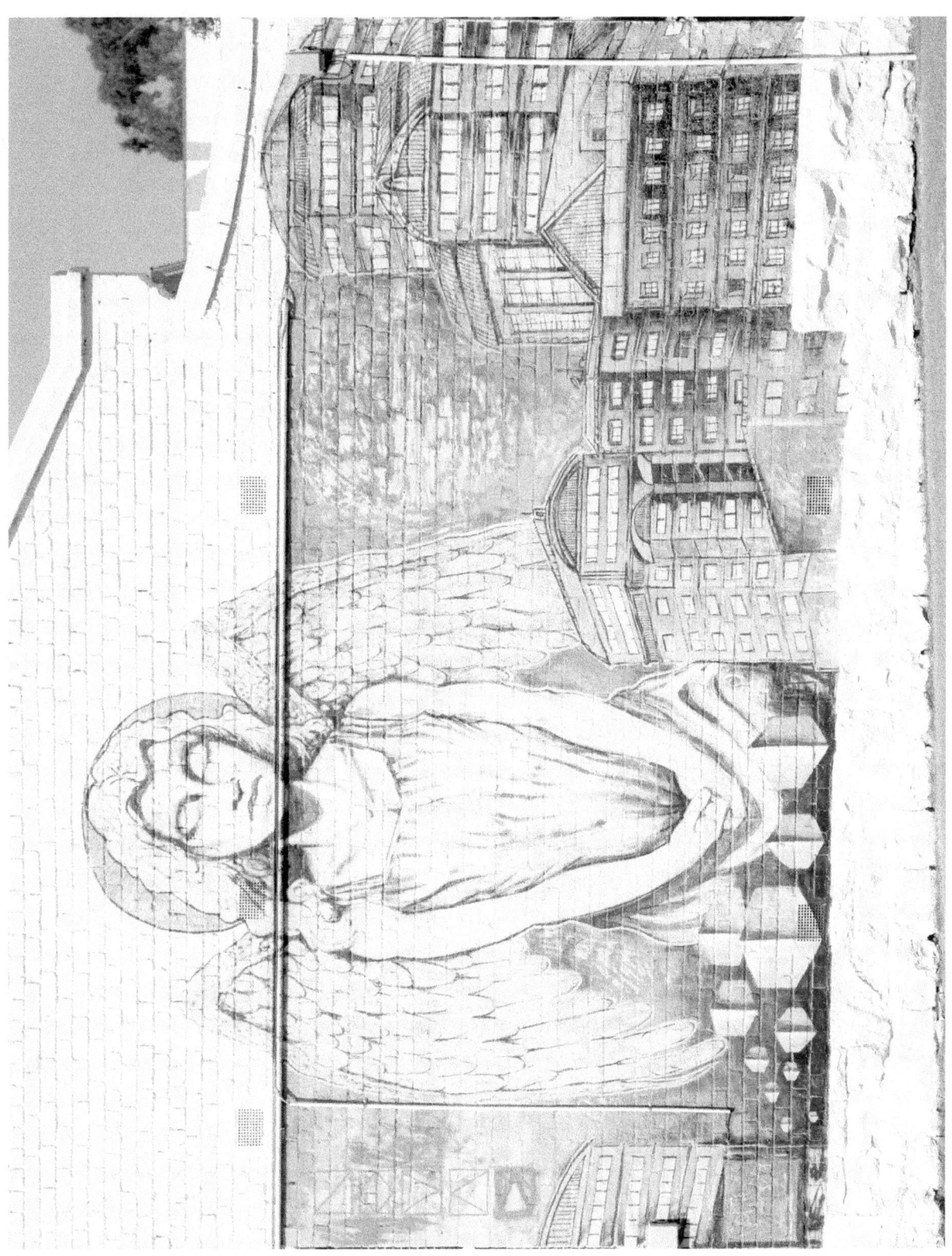

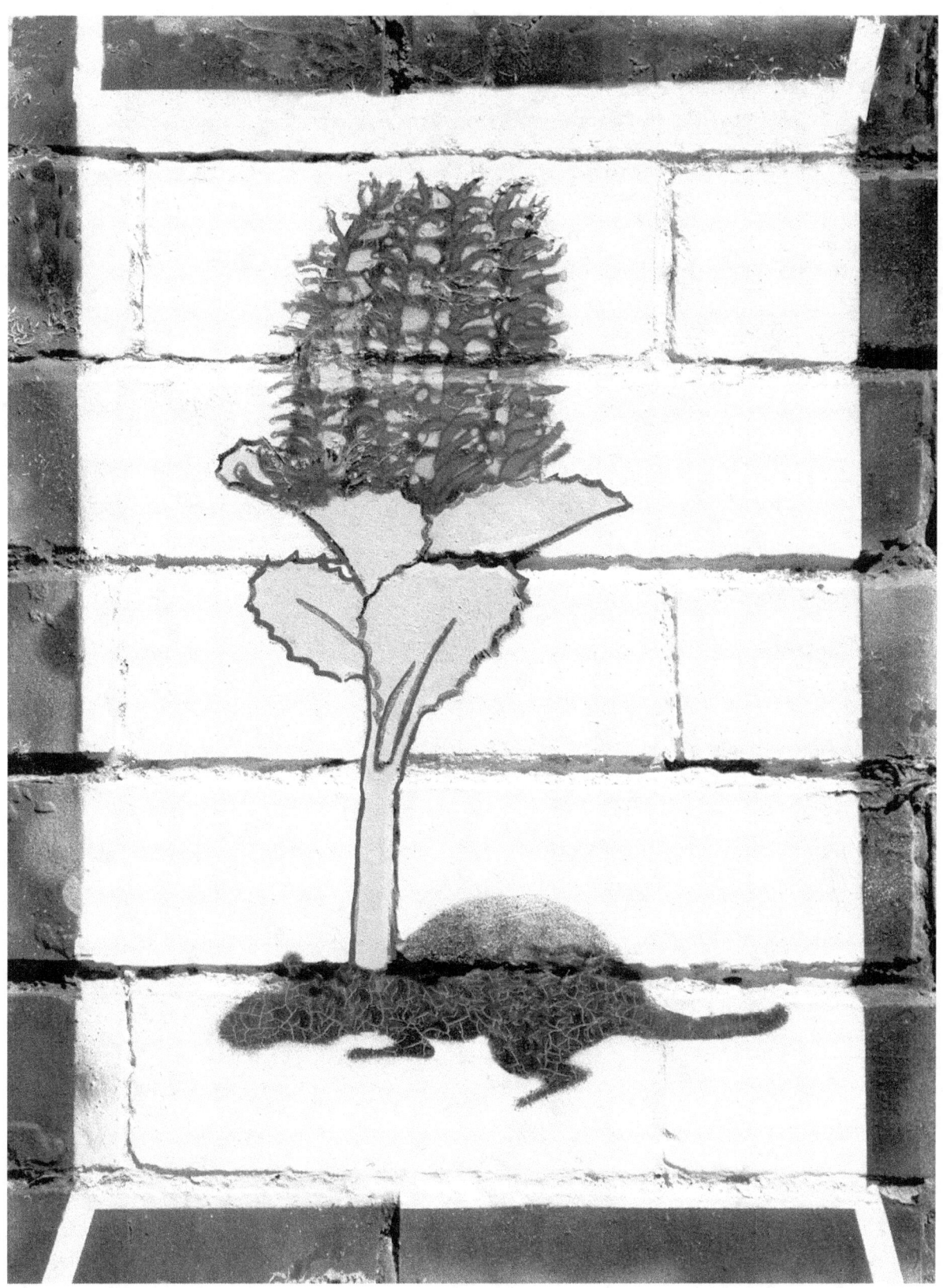

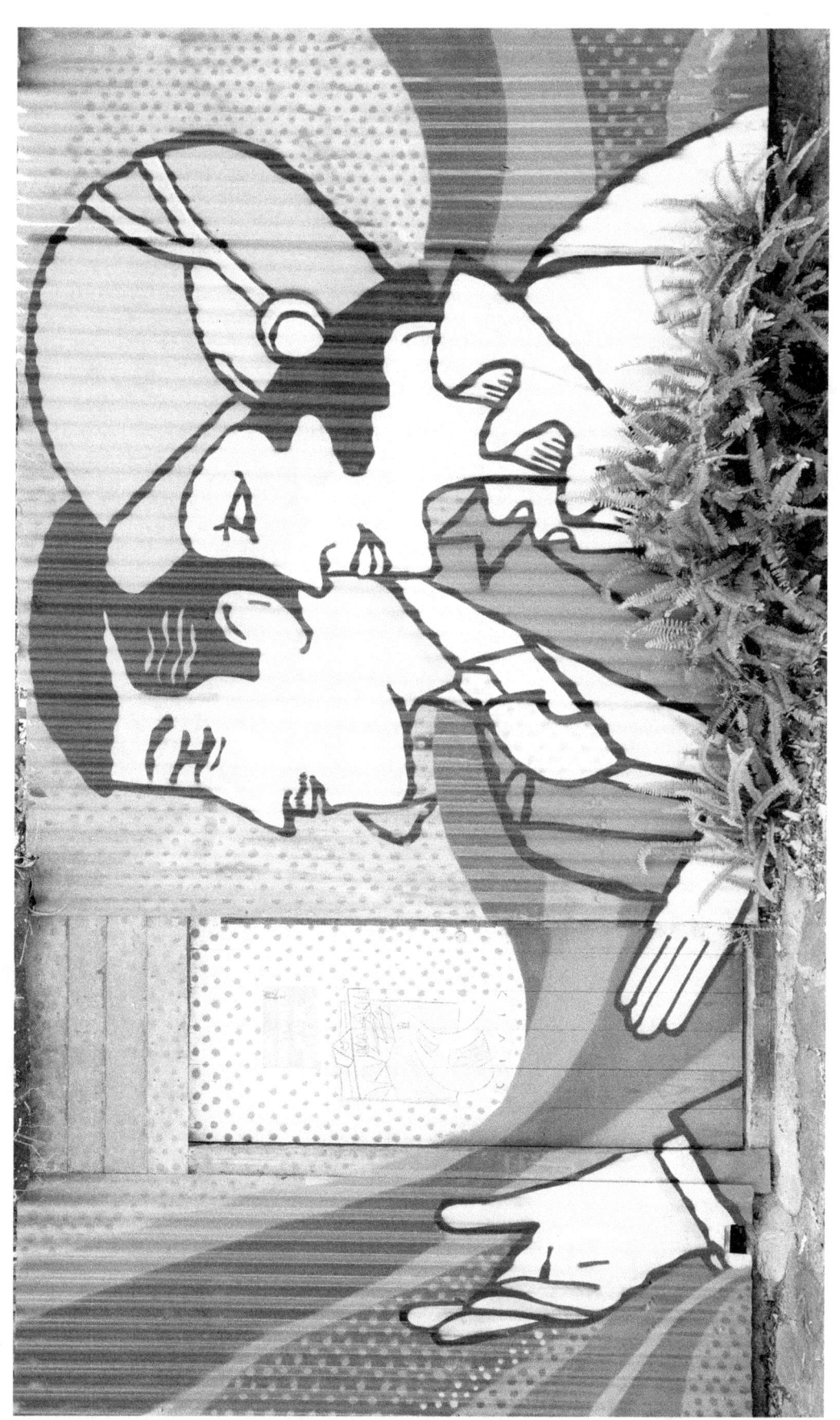

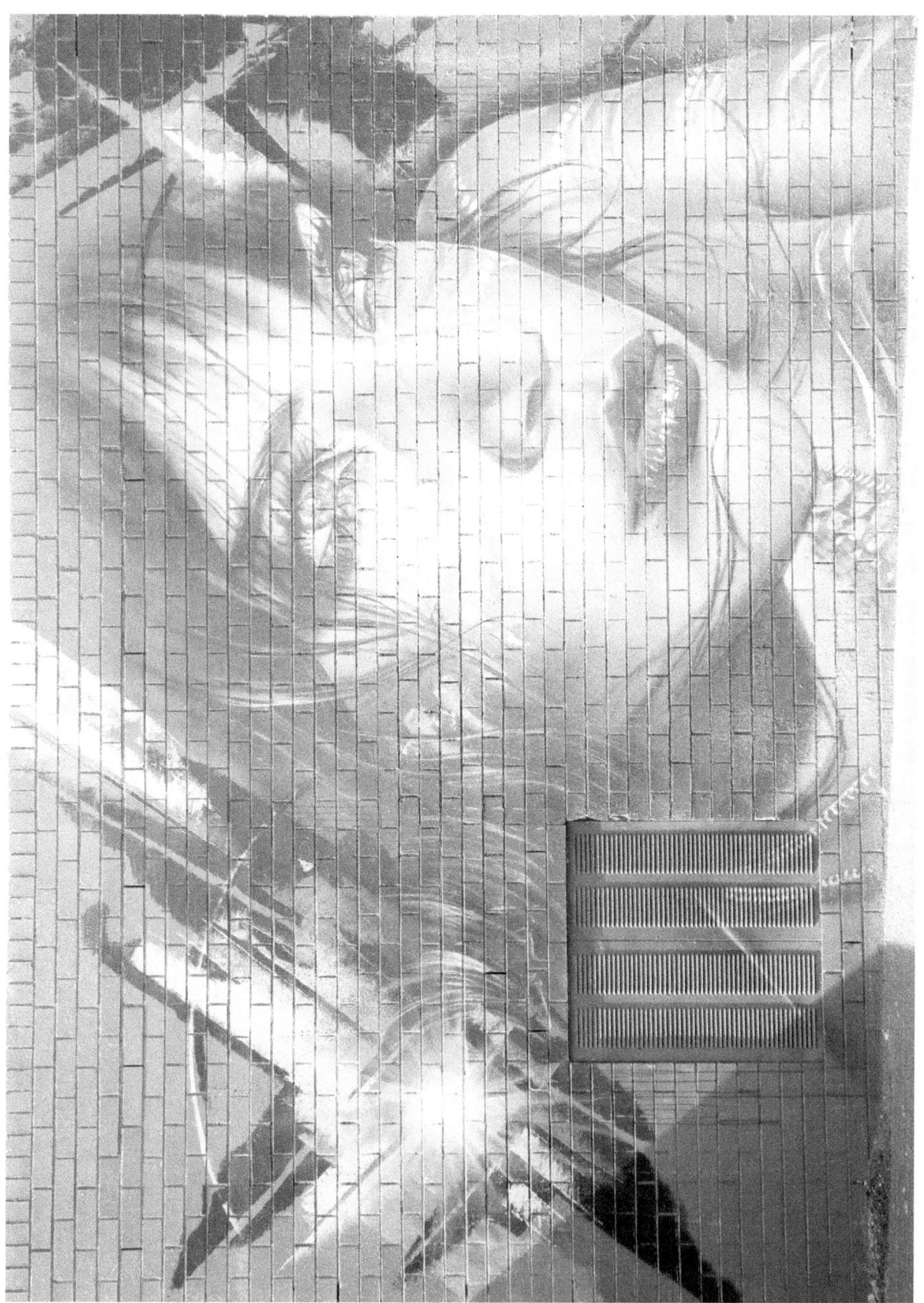

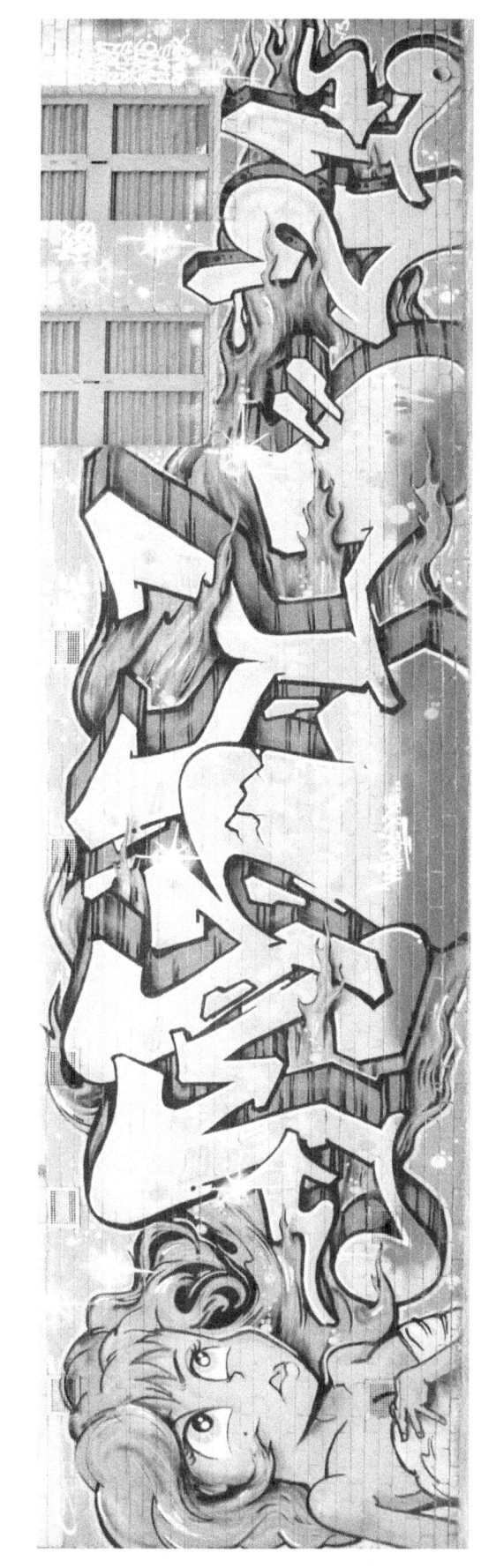

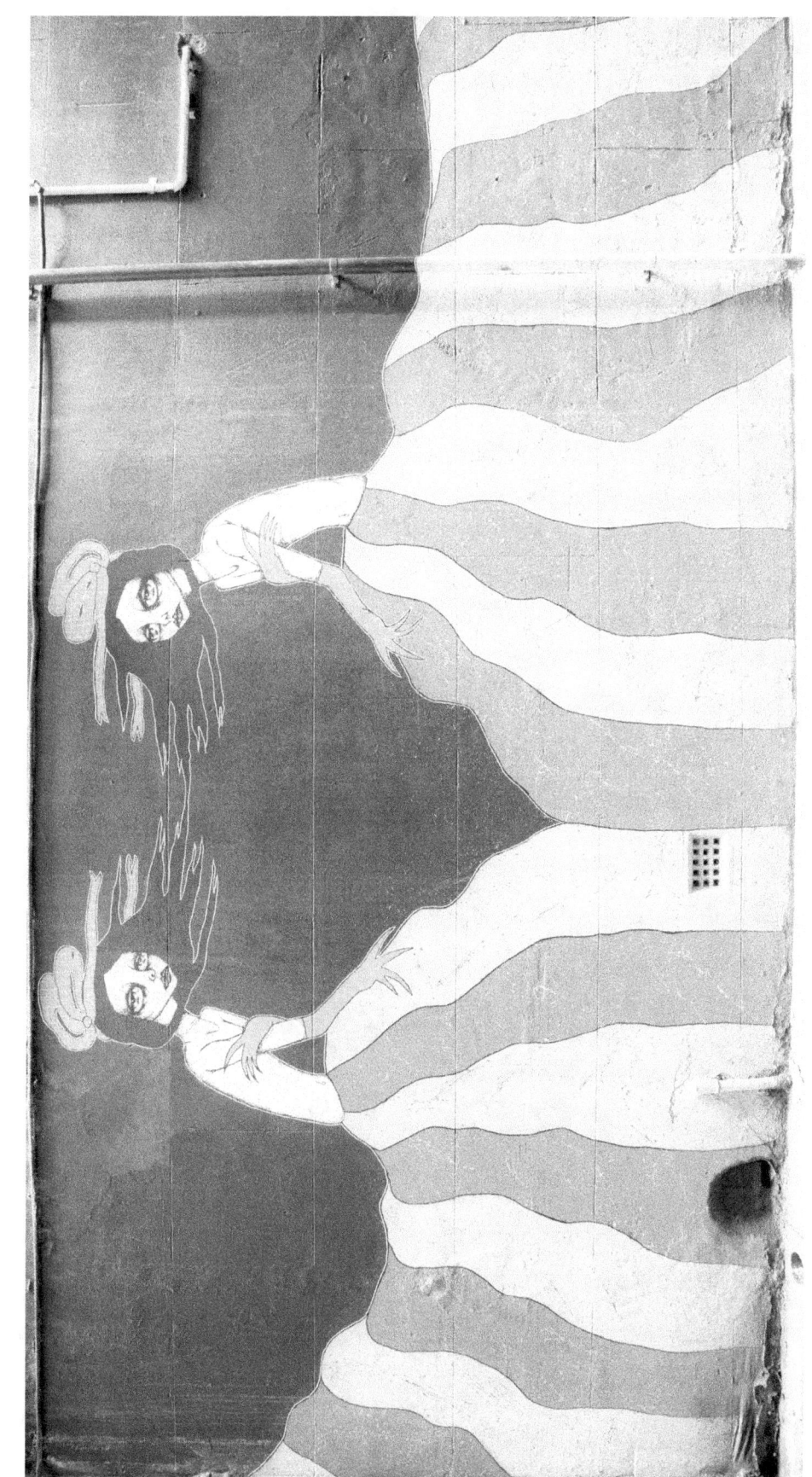

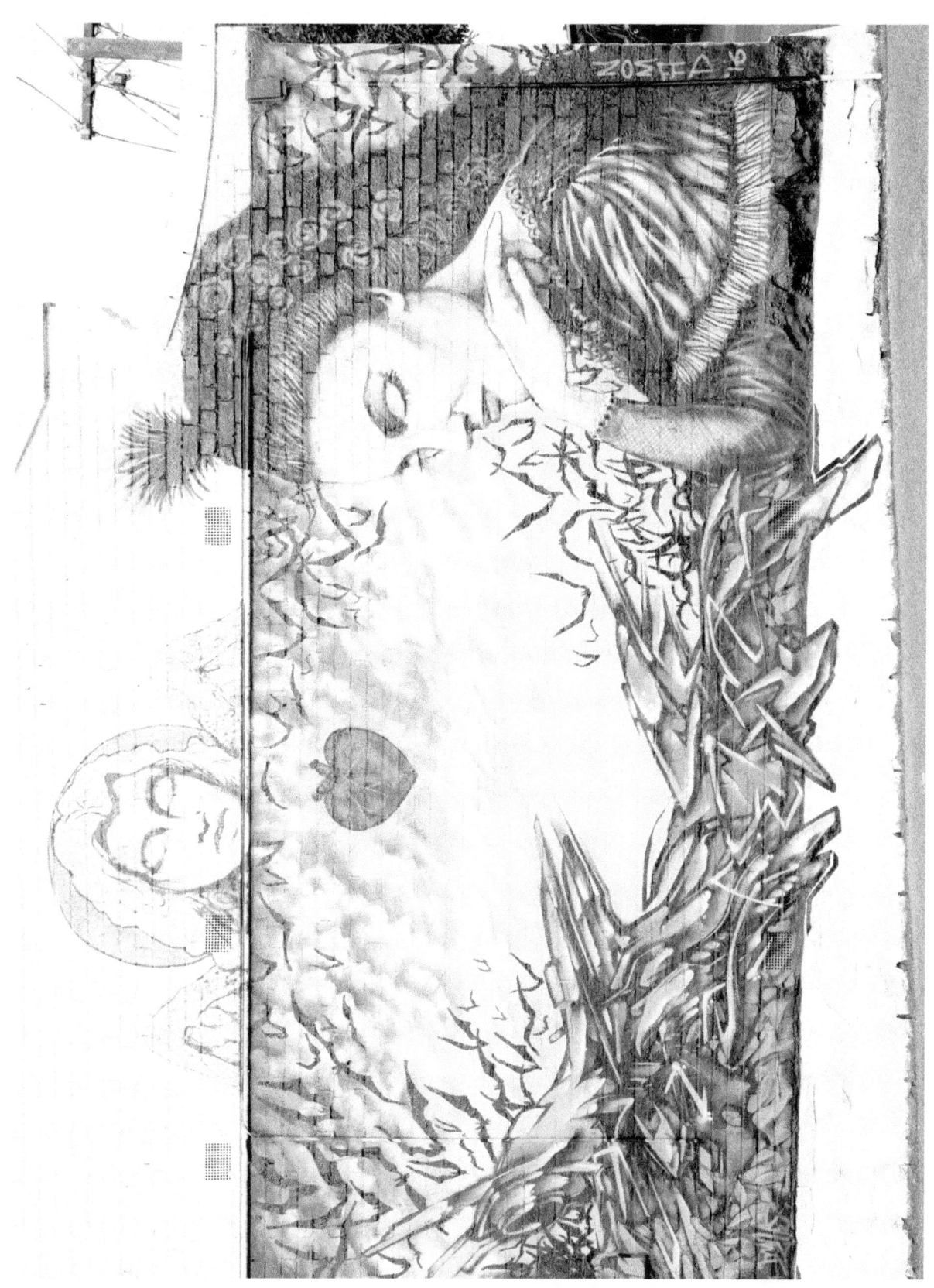

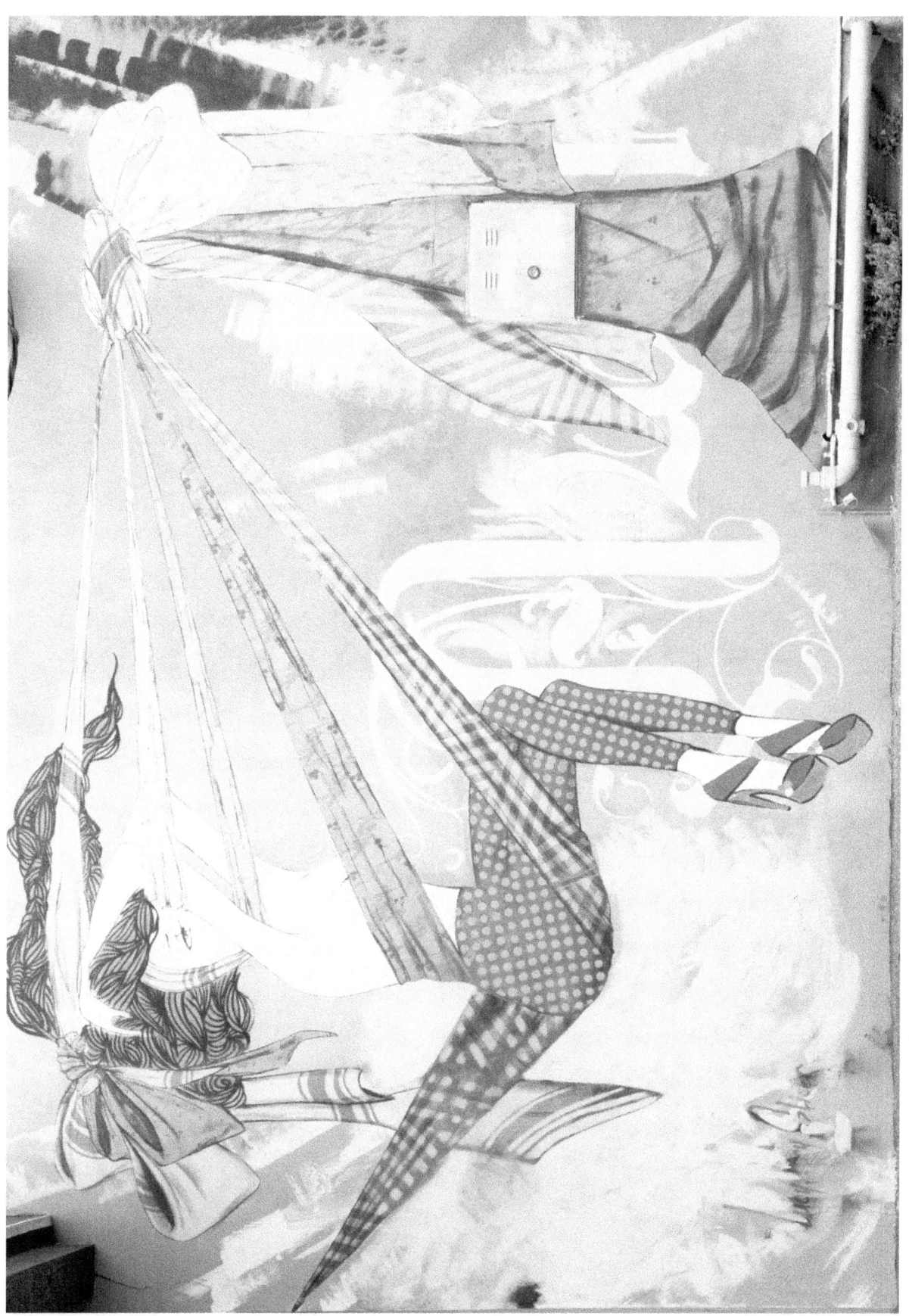

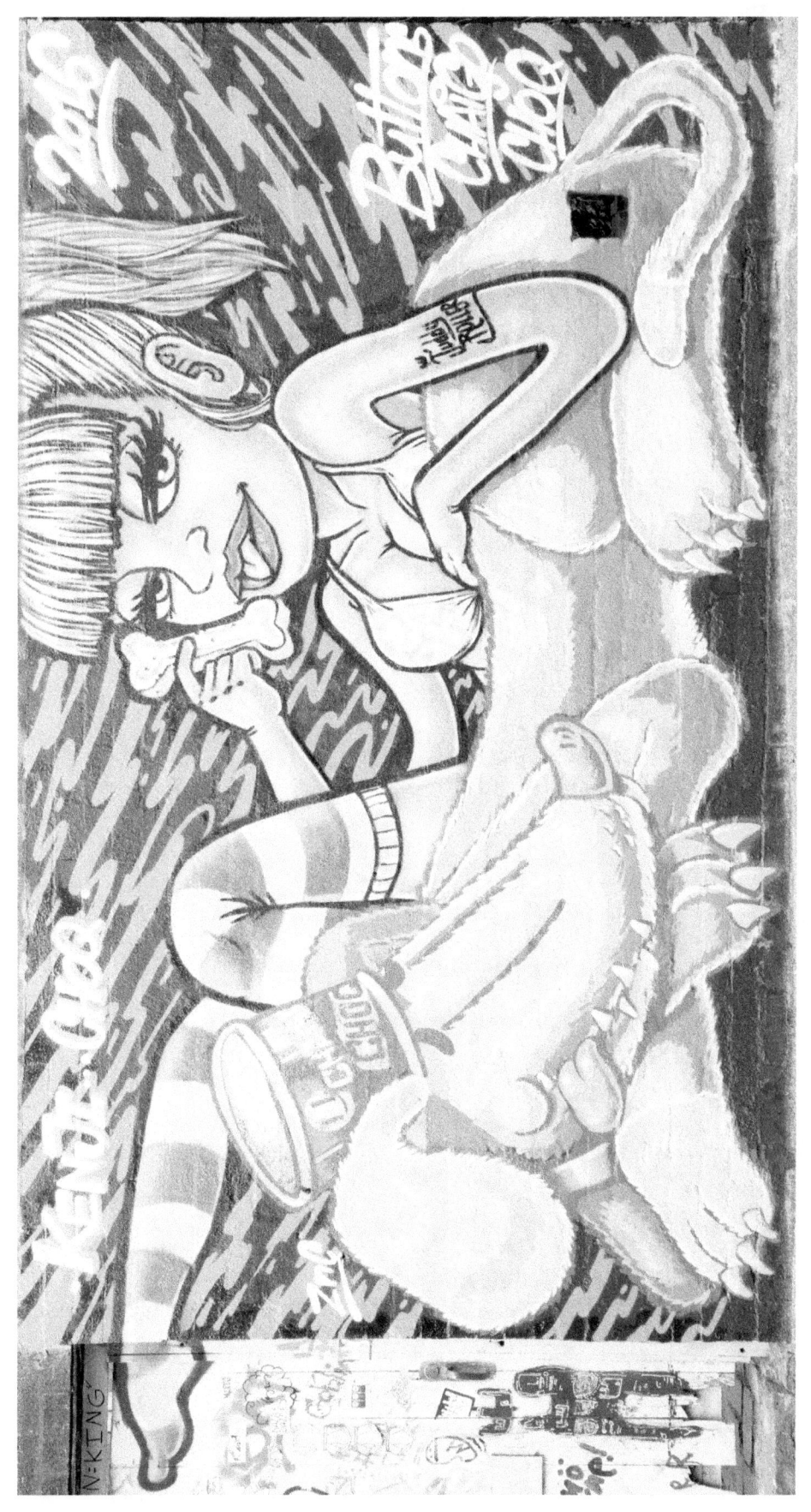

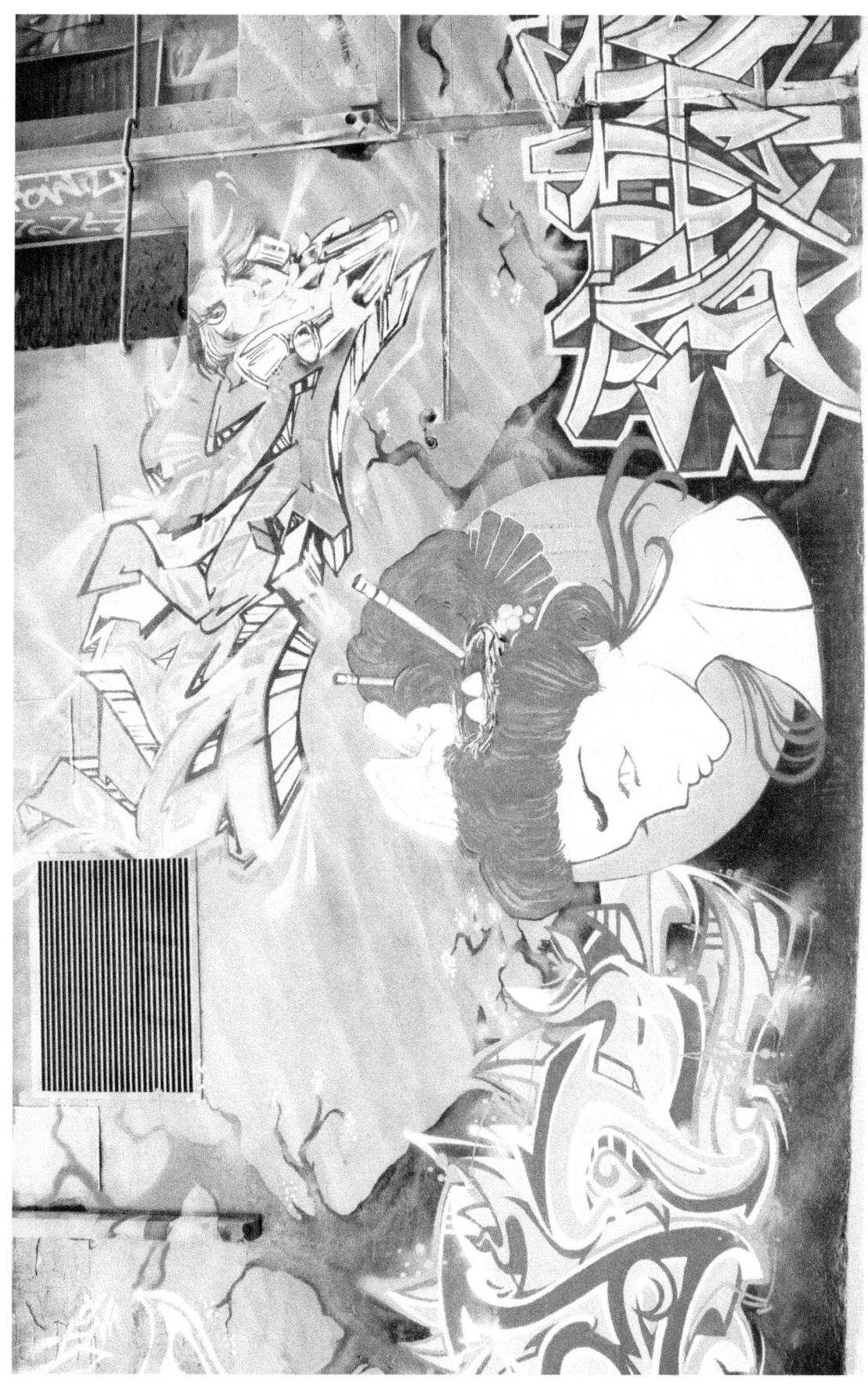

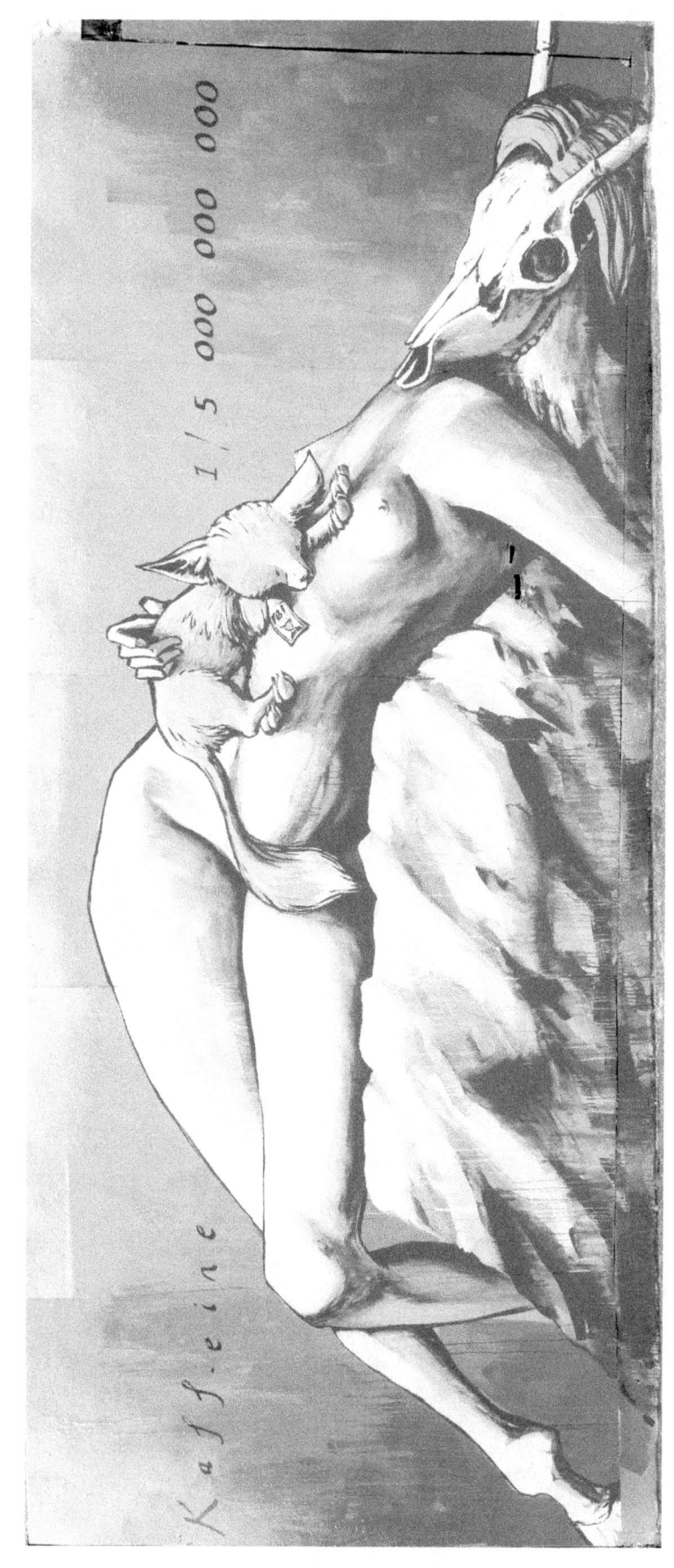

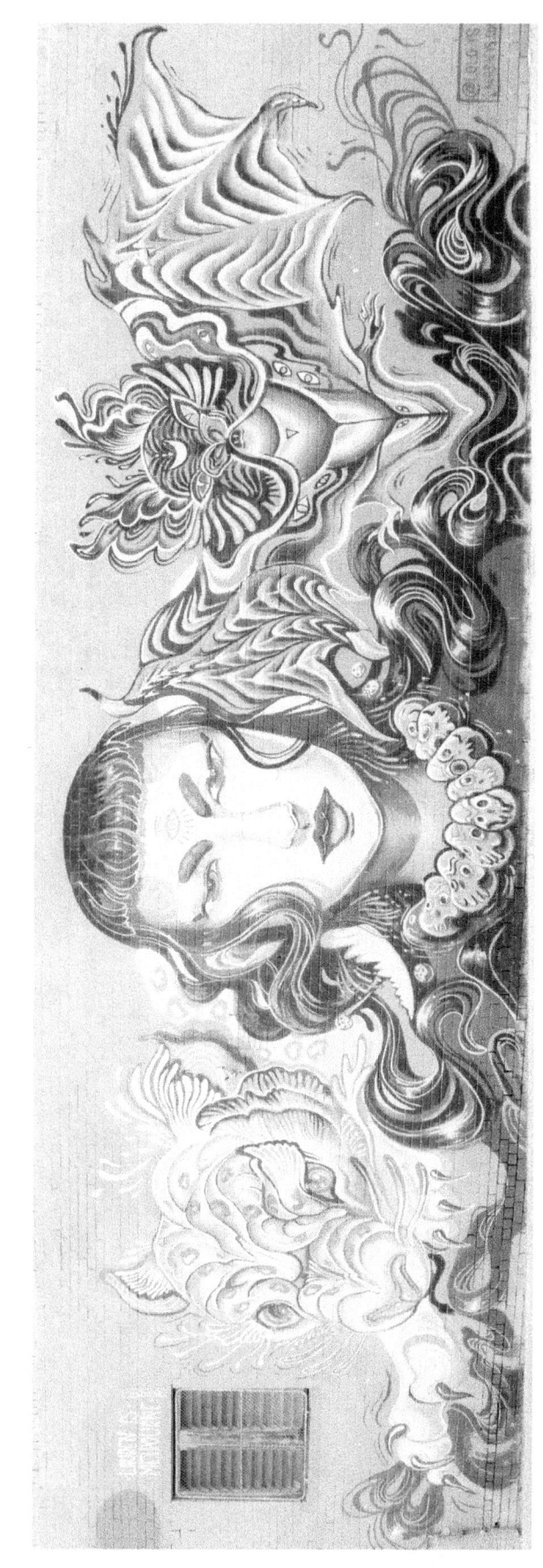

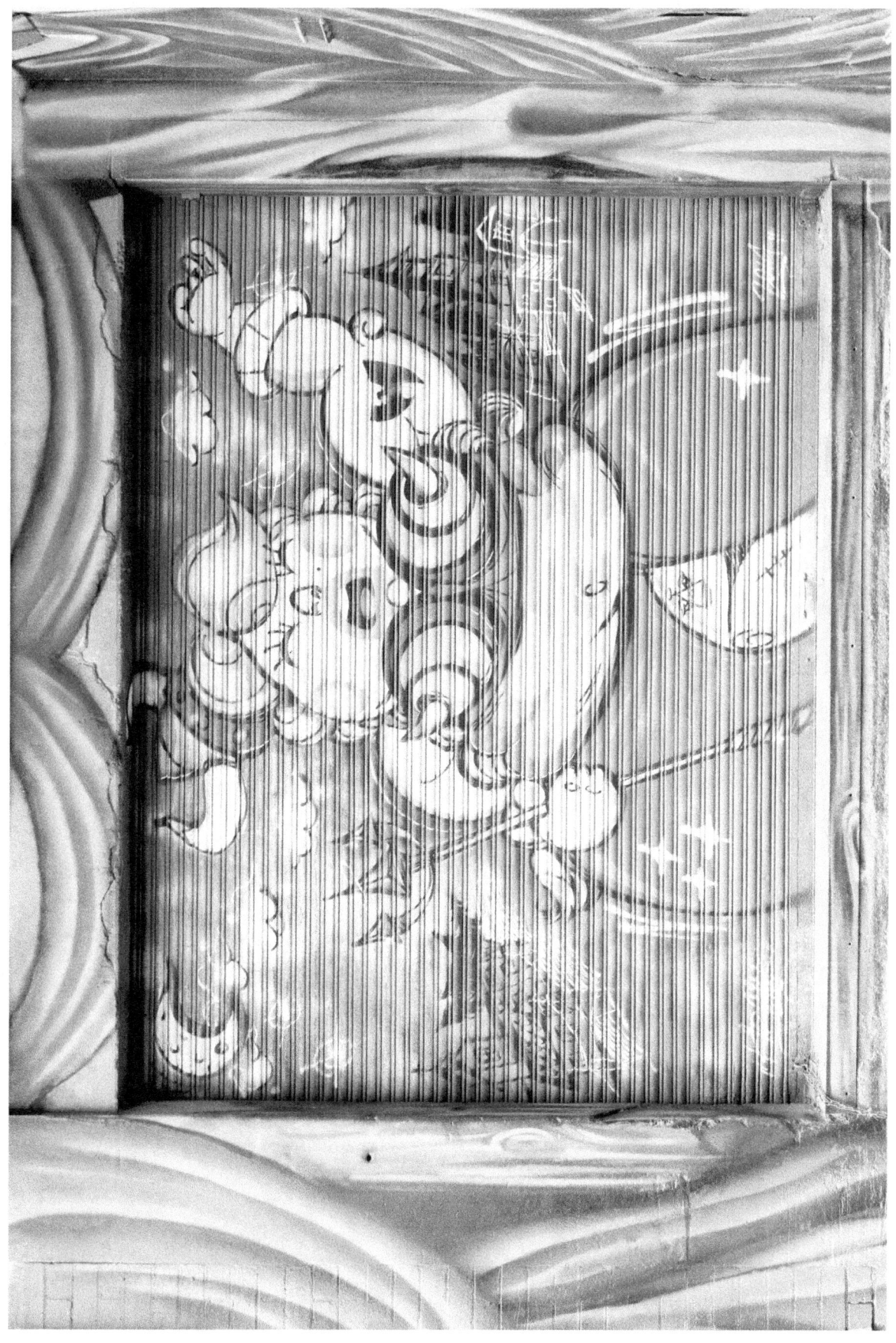

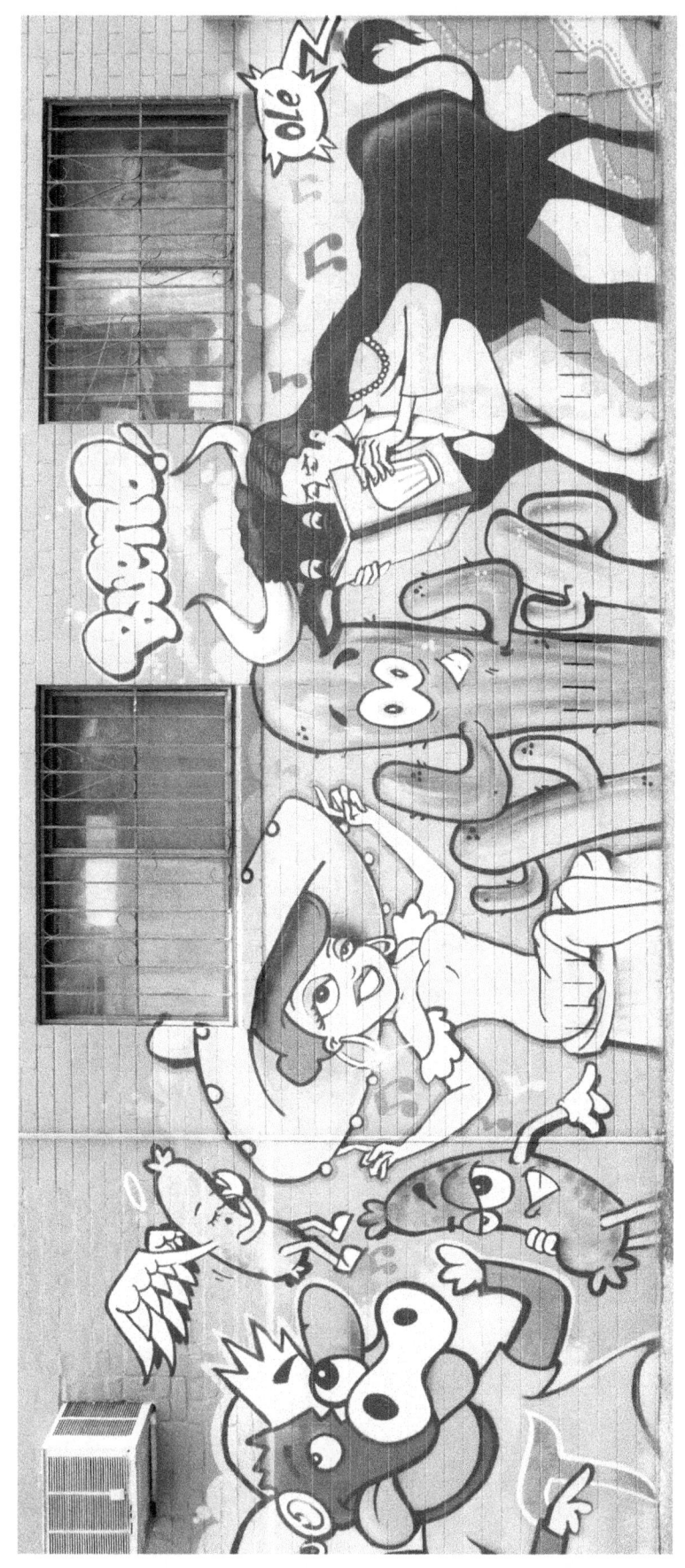

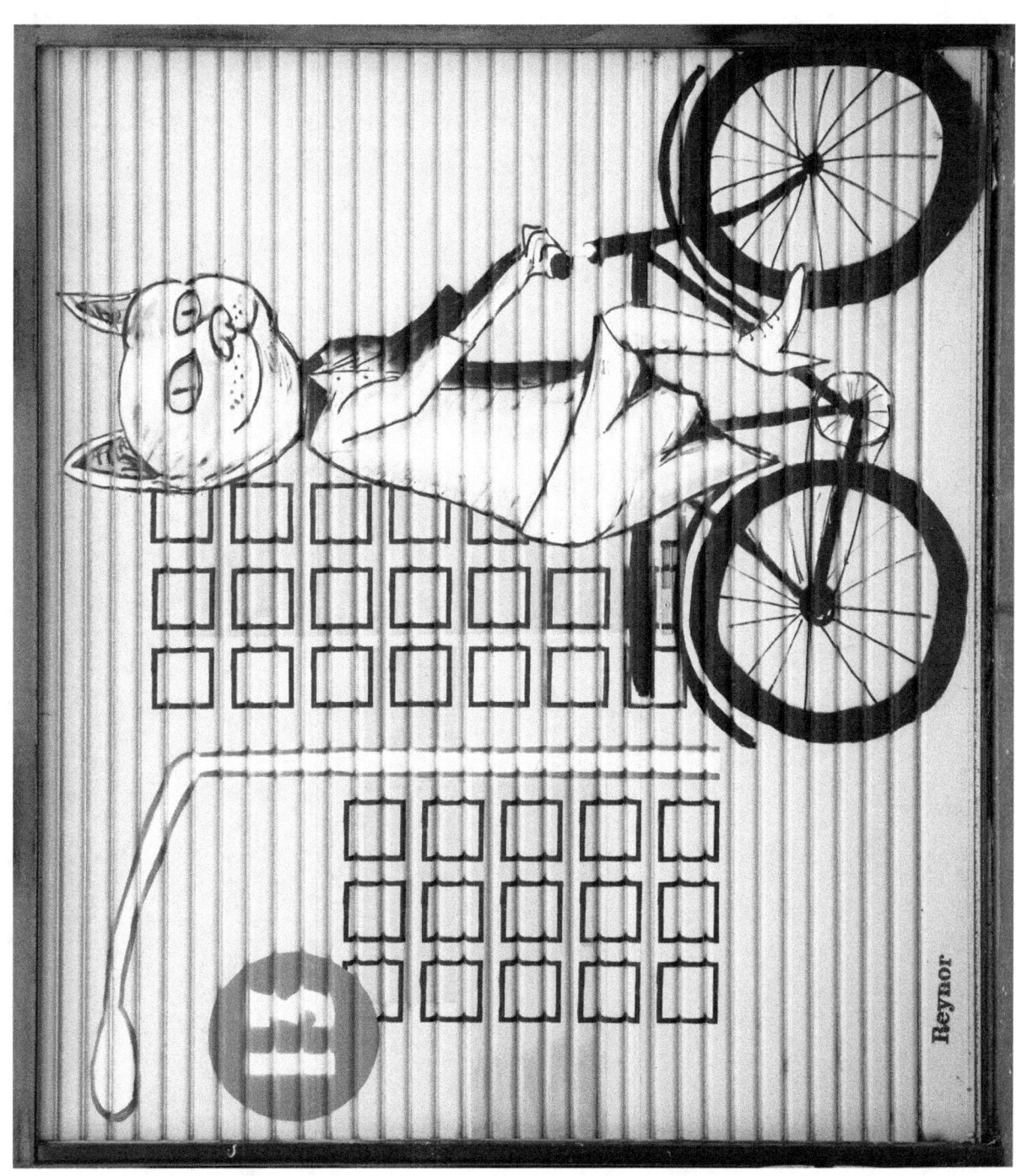

Reynor

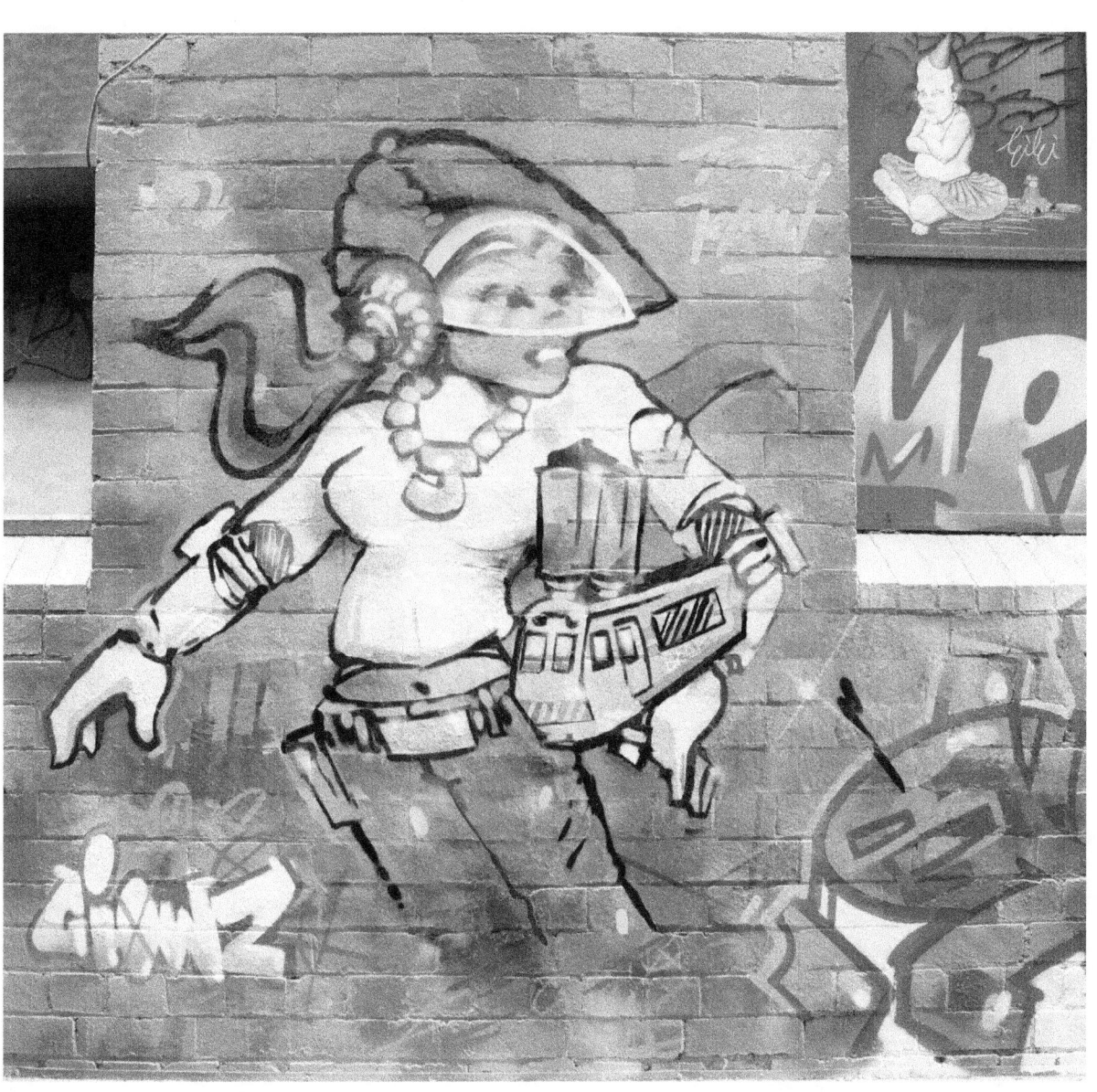

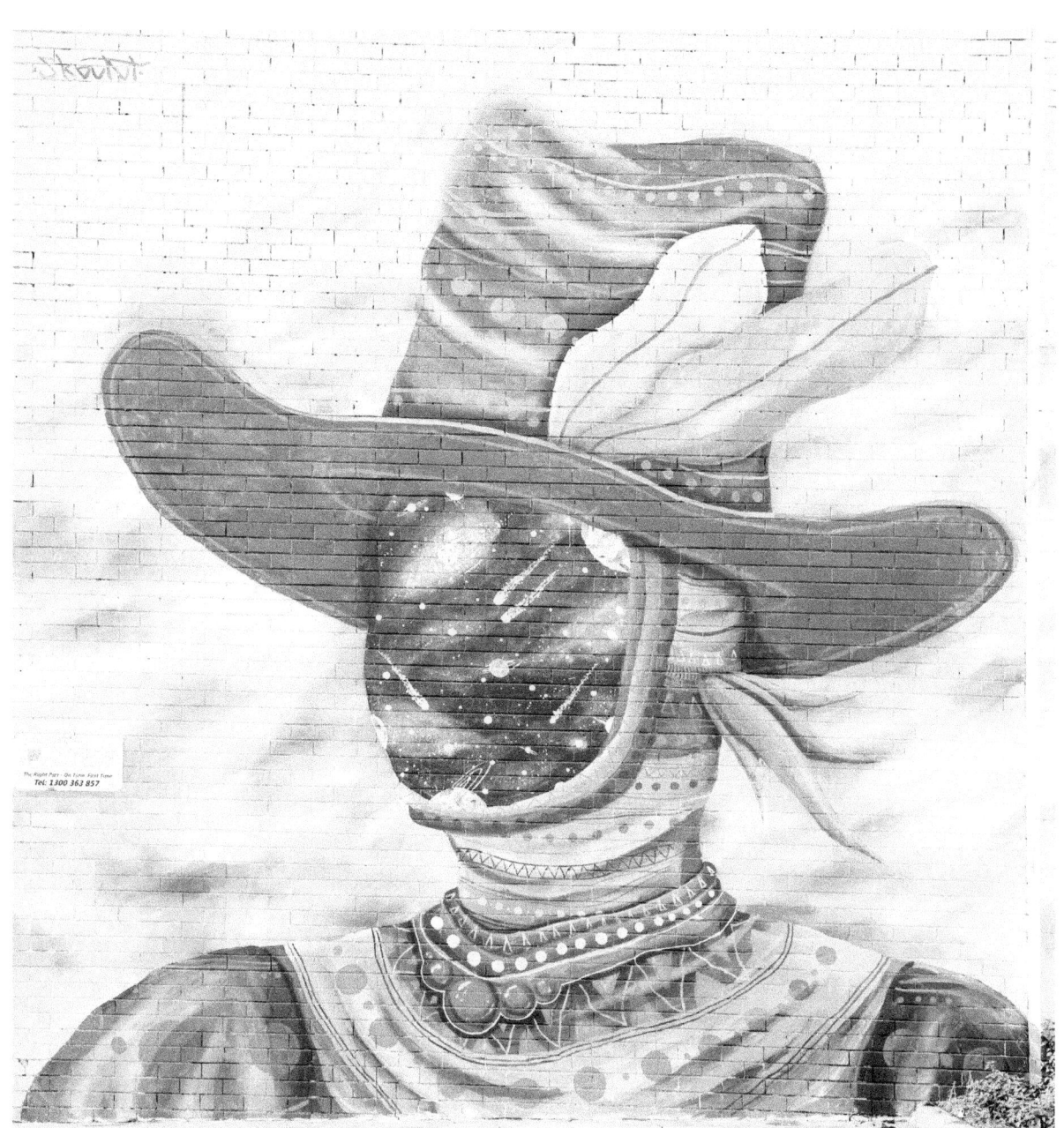

BLOTTING PAGE

BLOTTING PAGE